Stir

& PAN-FRY

RECIPES

The Family Circle® Promise of Success

Welcome to the world of Confident Cooking, created for you in the **Family Circle® Test Kitchen,** where recipes are double-tested by our team of home economists to achieve a high standard of success.

MURDOCH BOOKS®

Sydney • London • Vancouver • New York

Sensational Pan-fried Sandwiches

Pan-fried Cheese Sandwich

Spread 2 slices of bread with softened butter, covering the bread evenly all the way to the edges. Turn one slice over and spread the unbuttered side with wholegrain mustard. Place slices of ham and thinly sliced Gruyere cheese on top. Place the other slice of bread on top, unbuttered side down.

Heat a heavy-based frying pan and add the sandwich, cooking over medium heat 2 minutes or until underside is golden, and cheese is beginning to melt. Using a spatula, carefully turn sandwich over and fry until golden.

Pan-fried Cheese Sandwich

Italian-style Fried Sandwich

Spread 2 slices of white bread evenly with butter. Fill with thinly sliced mozzarella, finely shredded sundried tomato or capsicum and half a finely chopped anchovy fillet. Top with remaining bread, cut sandwich in half. Dip each sandwich in beaten egg. Drain excess and sprinkle lightly with sesame seeds.

Heat 1 cm of oil in heavy-based frying pan until moderately hot. Fry sandwiches 2—3 minutes each side until lightly golden. Drain on paper towels and serve immediately.

Italian-style Fried Sandwich

Sardine Fingers

Spread 2 slices white bread with butter. Turn one slice over and spread unbuttered side generously with mashed sardines in tomato sauce. Season with salt and pepper and top with remaining bread, buttered side out; remove crusts and cut into three portions. Fry in a heavy-based frying pan until lightly golden.

Sardine Finger

Gourmet Sandwich

Spread 2 slices of brown bread with softened butter. Turn one side over and spread unbuttered side with mashed avocado. Season with salt and pepper to taste. Cover with thin slices of cooked chicken breast, slices of tomato and slices of Camembert or Brie. Place the other slice of bread on top, unbuttered side up.

Heat a heavy-based frying pan and add the sandwich, cooking over medium heat 2 minutes or until underside is golden, and cheese is beginning to melt. Using a spatula, carefully turn sandwich over and fry until golden.

Gourmet Sandwich

Egg-wich

Spread 2 slices of bread with softened butter and cut a round from each slice using a large biscuit or scone cutter. Turn one round over and spread the unbuttered side with mayonnaise. Cook bread rounds, buttered-side down for 3 minutes or until golden. Quickly fry 1 egg in an egg ring in the same pan. When egg is almost cooked, return bread to pan briefly to re-heat. Place fried egg on the bread round which has been spread with mayonnaise. Season with salt and pepper and top with chopped chives and remaining bread round, cooked side up. Cut in half and serve immediately.

Egg-wich

Fruity French Toast

Lightly beat an egg with 1 tablespoon of milk. Dip slices of fruit bread into egg mixture, drain off excess, and fry in 2 tablespoons of butter until lightly golden on both sides. Cut bread in half and top with a scoop of ice-cream and a little maple syrup. Alternatively serve with jam.

Fruity French Toast

Stir-fry dishes

Here is a selection of quick, fresh and delicious meals from the frying pan or wok. Along with traditional Asian dishes, there are new and innovative recipes and combinations of ingredients.

Pork Chow Mein

Preparation time: 20 minutes
Total cooking time: 15 minutes
Serves 4

250 g fresh, thin egg noodles or Italian vermicelli
1 medium onion
1 medium carrot
4 spring onions
1 small red capsicum
1/3 cup oil
1 teaspoon finely chopped garlic
2 teaspoons finely chopped ginger
1 cup cubed cooked pork or ham
1 tablespoon hoisin sauce
1/2 cup bean sprouts, tails removed
3 teaspoons cornflour
1 1/4 cups chicken stock

1. Place noodles in a large pan of boiling water and cook until just tender. Drain and spread out on a clean tea towel to dry. Cut onion into quarters or eighths and separate the layers. Cut carrot into thin strips.
2. Cut spring onions into medium lengths and capsicums into small squares.
3. Heat 1 tablespoon of oil in a heavy-based frying pan. Add half the noodles and cook over moderate heat 5 minutes or until a golden, crisp cake has formed. Turn noodle cake over and cook another 5 minutes, drizzling another tablespoon of oil down the side of the pan while it cooks. Transfer noodles to a plate and keep warm. Repeat this procedure with the remaining noodles.

Honeyed Chicken with Cashews (top, recipe page 6) and Pork Chow Mein

4. Heat remaining oil in frying pan or wok and stir-fry garlic and ginger until lightly golden. Add onion, carrot, spring onion and capsicum and stir-fry over high heat for 3 minutes.
5. Add pork and hoisin sauce and cook, stirring occasionally, another minute. Add bean sprouts and toss for a few seconds.
6. Blend cornflour with a little of the stock. Add to pan. Add remaining stock. Stir until liquid boils and thickens. Use a knife to break up noodle cakes into serving portions. Spoon pork mixture over these portions. Serve immediately.

Honeyed Chicken with Cashews

Preparation time:
15 minutes
Total cooking time:
10 minutes
Serves 4

4 chicken breast fillets
2 medium onions
2 tablespoons oil
1/2 cup raw cashews
3/4 cup chicken stock
1 tablespoon honey
1 tablespoon cornflour
2 spring onions, diagonally sliced
salt or soy sauce, to taste

1. Cut chicken into long thin strips. Cut onions in half, then into thin wedges.
2. Heat half the oil in wok or heavy-based pan; add nuts. Stir-fry over high heat for 2 minutes or until nuts are golden. Remove from pan and drain on paper towels. Heat remaining oil; add onion and stir-fry over high heat 2 minutes or until slightly wilted.
3. Add chicken; stir-fry 4 minutes or until browned. Reduce heat to low; add half the stock and cook until chicken is tender and stock has almost reduced away.
4. Combine nuts, honey, remaining stock and cornflour in a small bowl. Pour over chicken; stir until sauce has lightly thickened. Sprinkle with sliced spring onion and season with salt or soy sauce, to taste. Garnish with red capsicum strips, if desired.

> HINT
> Do not overcook stir-fries. Vegetables, in particular, should be only just tender, retaining most of their crispness.

Lamb Stir-fry with Mixed Greens

Preparation time:
10 minutes
Total cooking time:
15 minutes
Serves 4

500 g lamb fillets
salt and pepper, to taste
1 egg white, lightly beaten
1 tablespoon cornflour
2–3 tablespoons oil
2 cm piece fresh ginger, thinly sliced
2 cloves garlic, crushed
2 tablespoons soy sauce
2 medium sized leeks, finely sliced
250 g young fresh English spinach leaves, washed and torn
1 small bunch bok choy, cut into pieces about 2.5 cm long
3/4 cup frozen peas
1 teaspoon sugar
1/4 cup chicken stock
dash chilli sauce

1. Cut the lamb into diagonal strips, about 2.5 cm wide. Sprinkle meat with salt and pepper, dip in egg white and dust with cornflour. Heat half the oil in a frying pan or wok; add ginger, garlic and soy sauce and stir-fry over high heat 30 seconds. Add lamb;

Lamb Stir-fry with Mixed Greens

stir-fry over high heat 1 minute or until meat has changed colour. Reduce the heat to medium; cover pan and cook for 3 minutes. Remove meat from pan.
2. Heat remaining oil; add leek. Stir-fry over high heat 3 minutes or until the leek becomes limp.
3. Add spinach, bok choy and frozen peas; stir-fry 1 minute. Reduce heat and cover pan; cook 2 minutes. Combine sugar, stock and chilli in a small bowl; add to pan and stir through. Add lamb and stir until mixed; cook 2 minutes or until the lamb is tender and vegetables are just tender. Garnish with lemon zest, if desired.

Thai-style Beef

Preparation time:
15 minutes
Total cooking time:
7 minutes
Serves 4

200 g dried egg noodles
400 g beef eye fillet
2 tablespoons oil
1 red capsicum, cut into strips
2 cloves garlic, crushed
500 g baby bok choy, chopped
8 spring onions, chopped
1/4 cup lime juice
2 tablespoons sweet chilli sauce
2 tablespoons Thai fish sauce
1/4 cup chopped fresh coriander
1/4 cup chopped fresh mint

1. Cook noodles in boiling water according to instructions on the packet; drain.
2. Slice beef evenly across the grain into flat, thin strips.
3. Heat half the oil in a frying pan or wok; add beef in batches. Stir-fry each batch quickly over high heat until browned but not cooked through. Remove from pan; drain on paper towels.
4. Heat remaining oil in the same pan; add capsicum and garlic and stir-fry over high heat 1 minute. Add bok choy and spring onion; stir-fry over high heat for 2 minutes.
5. Add lime juice, chilli sauce, fish sauce, coriander, mint, noodles and beef; stir-fry over high heat 2 minutes or until heated through.

Coconut Thai Vegetables

Preparation time:
15 minutes
Total cooking time:
15 minutes
Serves 4–6

1 tablespoon oil
2 small onions, cut in wedges
1 teaspoon ground cumin
150 g cauliflower florets
1 medium red capsicum, chopped
2 sticks celery, sliced diagonally
1 1/2 cups grated pumpkin (375 g)
1 cup coconut milk
1 cup vegetable stock
1 tablespoon sweet chilli sauce
150 g green beans
1 tablespoon finely chopped fresh coriander

1. Heat oil in frying pan or wok. Add onion and cumin; stir over medium heat 2 minutes or until onion is golden.
2. Add cauliflower; stir-fry over high heat for 2 minutes; add capsicum, celery and pumpkin and stir-fry over high heat 2 minutes or until the vegetables have begun to soften.
3. Add coconut milk, vegetable stock and chilli sauce; bring to boil. Reduce heat and cook, uncovered, 8 minutes or until the vegetables are almost tender.
4. Trim tops and tails of beans and cut in half. Add beans and coriander to pan; cook another 2 minutes or until beans are just tender. Remove from heat. Serve with steamed rice, if desired.

Hint
Stir-fry meat in batches to avoid overcrowding the pan or wok. Overcrowded meat will release juice that will stew the meat and toughen it.

Thai-style Beef (top)
Coconut Thai Vegetables

Snow Peas with Capsicum

Preparation time:
10 minutes
Total cooking time:
7 minutes
Serves 4

1 large onion, peeled
185 g snow peas
1 tablespoon oil
1 tablespoon grated ginger
1 red capsicum, cut into strips
1 small clove garlic, crushed
1 tablespoon oyster sauce
1 teaspoon sugar
pinch salt
1 tablespoon water

1. Cut onion in half; slice thinly. Remove ends and threads from snow peas.
2. Heat oil in frying pan or wok; add onion, ginger and capsicum and stir-fry over high heat 4–5 minutes or until vegetables are just tender. Add garlic and snow peas; stir-fry for 2 minutes until snow peas become bright green.
3. Add oyster sauce, sugar, salt and water to pan and mix through. Serve immediately.

Coconut Prawns with Bamboo Shoots

Preparation time:
20 minutes
Total cooking time:
5 minutes
Serves 4

1.25 kg uncooked king prawns
2 tablespoons oil
2 onions, cut into wedges
1–2 tablespoons green curry paste
230 g can sliced bamboo shoots, drained
1/2 cup coconut milk
1 tablespoon lemon juice
3 teaspoons fish sauce
2 teaspoons sugar
1/3 cup chopped fresh basil

1. Peel and devein prawns, leaving the tails intact. Heat oil in pan; add onion, stir-fry over medium heat 3 minutes or until soft. Add curry paste; stir-fry over high heat 1 minute. Add prawns; stir-fry over high heat 1 minute.
2. Add bamboo shoots, coconut milk, juice, fish sauce, sugar and basil; stir-fry over high heat 2 minutes or until sauce has thickened.

From top: Snow Peas with Capsicum, Coconut Prawns with Bamboo Shoots and Stir-fried Asparagus with Sesame Seeds

Stir-fried Asparagus with Sesame Seeds

Preparation time:
10 minutes
Total cooking time:
6 minutes
Serves 4

1 tablespoon sesame seeds
2 tablespoons oil
1 clove garlic, finely chopped
1 teaspoon grated fresh ginger
750 g asparagus, trimmed and cut into 5 cm pieces
1 teaspoon salt
1/2 teaspoon pepper
1/2 teaspoon sugar
2 teaspoons sesame oil
1 tablespoon soy sauce

1. Heat wok or frying pan; add the sesame seeds and stir-fry over high heat 2 minutes or until golden. Remove from pan.
2. Heat oil in pan; add garlic, ginger and asparagus. Stir-fry over high heat 3 minutes or until almost tender. Sprinkle vegetables with salt and pepper; add sugar. Stir-fry over high heat 1 minute.
3. Sprinkle with sesame oil, soy sauce and sesame seeds. Serve immediately.

Beef and Bok Choy

Preparation time:
20 minutes
Total cooking time:
10 minutes
Serves 4

1 bunch bok choy
2 tablespoons oil
2 cloves garlic, crushed
250 g rump steak, thinly sliced
2 tablespoons soy sauce
1 tablespoon sweet sherry
2 tablespoons chopped fresh basil
2 teaspoons sesame oil

1. Wash bok choy; drain. Cut leaves into wide strips. Cut stems into thin strips. Heat 1 tablespoon oil in a frying pan or wok; add garlic and stir-fry 30 seconds.

2. Heat remaining oil; add meat in small batches and stir-fry 3 minutes over high heat until meat has browned but not cooked through. Remove meat from pan.

3. Stir-fry bok choy 30 seconds or until just wilted. Add meat, soy sauce and sherry. Stir-fry 2–3 minutes or until meat is tender.

4. Add basil and sesame oil; toss well. Serve immediately. Garnish with red capsicum strips, if desired.

Hint
The Asian vegetable, choi sum, has a similar flavour to bok choy and could be substituted in the above dish. It has a longer leaf and shorter stem. Baby bok choy could also be used.

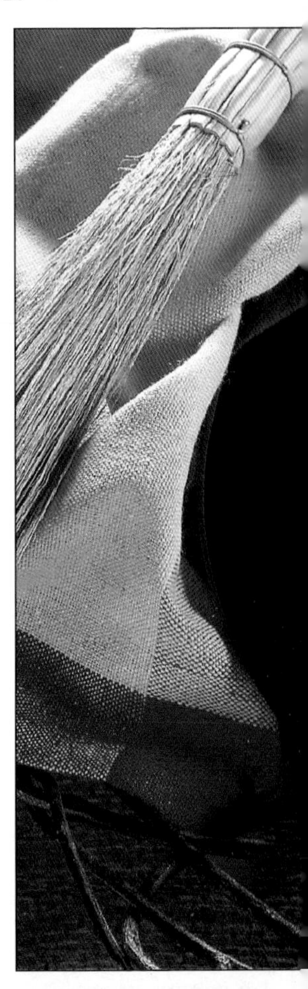

Beef and Bok Choy

1 Cut the leaves of bok choy into wide strips; cut stalks into thin strips.

2 Stir-fry beef in small batches over high heat until the meat has just browned.

3 Stir-fry bok choy briefly until the leaves have just begun to wilt.

4 Return meat to pan and add chopped fresh basil.

Fragrant Seafood Stir-fry

Preparation time:
20 minutes
Total cooking time:
5 minutes
Serves 4

400 g firm white fish fillets
200 g medium uncooked prawns
1 tablespoon oil
2 small red chillies, finely chopped
4 cm stalk lemon grass, white part only, finely chopped
2 cloves garlic, crushed
100 g snow peas, sliced diagonally
1–2 tablespoons fish sauce
6 spring onions, cut into 2 cm lengths
1/4 cup chopped basil
2 tablespoons chopped coriander

1. Cut fish into small cubes. Peel and devein prawns, leaving tails intact. Heat oil in heavy-based pan or wok; add chopped chilli, fish, lemon grass, garlic and snow peas. Stir-fry over medium heat 2 minutes or until fish has almost cooked. Add prawns; stir-fry 2 minutes or until prawns are pink.
2. Add sauce, onions, basil and coriander; stir-fry 1 minute. Serve immediately.

Mixed Ginger Vegetables

Preparation time:
10 minutes
Total cooking time:
5 minutes
Serves 4

1 tablespoon oil
3 teaspoons grated ginger
4 spring onions, sliced
230 g can water chestnuts, drained, halved
425 g can baby corn, drained
1 cup finely sliced Chinese cabbage
125 g bean sprouts, tails removed
1 tablespoon soy sauce
1–2 tablespoons oyster sauce
2 teaspoons sesame oil

1. Heat oil in heavy-based pan or wok; add ginger and spring onion. Stir-fry over high heat 1 minute. Add water chestnuts and baby corn; stir-fry 30 seconds.
2. Add cabbage, bean sprouts and sauces; stir-fry 1 minute. Stir in sesame oil; toss well.

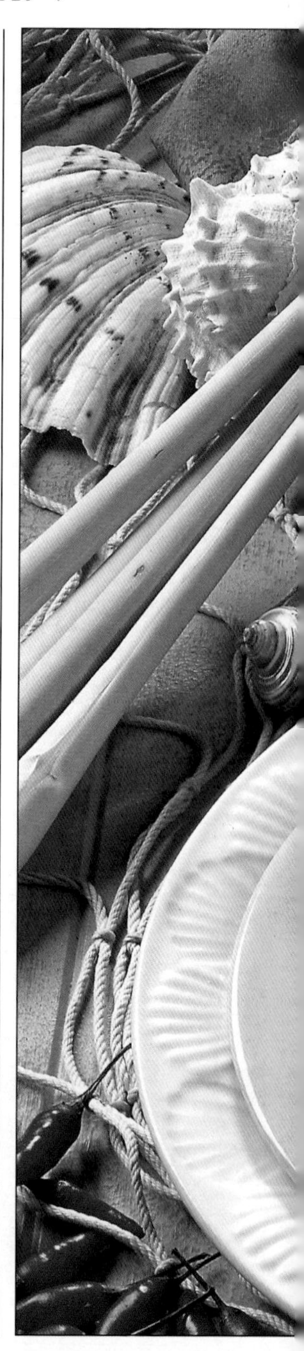

Mixed Ginger Vegetables (top) and Seafood Stir-fry

Chicken with Asparagus and Almonds

Preparation time:
15 minutes
Total cooking time:
8 minutes
Serves 4

500 g chicken thigh fillets
2 tablespoons oil
300 g fresh asparagus, cut into 5 cm lengths
1 large red capsicum, cut into strips
1 tablespoon grated fresh ginger
8 spring onions, cut into 3 cm lengths
2 teaspoons sweet chilli sauce
3 teaspoons soy sauce
1/2 cup blanched almonds, toasted

1. Trim chicken of excess fat and sinew. Cut into thin strips. Heat oil in frying pan or wok; add asparagus and capsicum and stir-fry over high heat 2 minutes. Remove from pan and set aside. Add ginger to pan; stir-fry 1 minute. Add chicken and stir-fry, in batches, 2–3 minutes or until golden brown. Return asparagus and capsicum to pan.
2. Add spring onion and sauces; stir-fry 2 minutes or until chicken and vegetables are tender. Add almonds and stir.

Note: If asparagus spears are thick, cut in half lengthways so they will cook more quickly.

Greek-style Lamb

Preparation time:
20 minutes
Total cooking time:
8 minutes
Serves 4

400 g lamb fillets
2 tablespoons olive oil
1 large red onion, sliced
3 medium zucchini, thinly sliced
200 g cherry tomatoes, halved
3 cloves garlic, crushed
2 tablespoons lemon juice
1/3 cup pitted black olives, halved
2 tablespoons fresh oregano, finely chopped
100 g feta cheese, crumbled
1/3 cup pine nuts, toasted

1. Cut the lamb fillets across the grain into thin strips. Heat the pan or wok, then add olive oil and heat for 30 seconds. Add lamb strips in small batches and stir-fry each batch over high heat for 1–2 minutes or until browned. Transfer to a plate.
2. Add onion and zucchini to pan or wok. Stir-fry over high heat 2 minutes or until just tender. Add cherry tomatoes and crushed garlic. Stir-fry for 1–2 minutes until tomatoes have just softened. Return the meat to the pan and stir over high heat until heated through.
3. Remove pan from heat. Add juice, olives and oregano to pan and toss until well combined. Sprinkle with crumbled feta cheese and pine nuts before serving.

> **Hint**
> Stir-fries do not have to be limited to traditional Asian ingredients. You can experiment with foods such as olives, tomatoes and cheese, for example. As long as they are fresh and cooked quickly they will make a delicious, interesting meal.

Chicken with Asparagus and Almonds (top)
Greek-style Lamb

Sweet and Spicy Steak and Vegetables

Preparation time: 15 minutes
Total cooking time: 10 minutes
Serves 4

500 g beef eye fillet
2 tablespoons oil
2 carrots, thinly sliced
2 teaspoons sesame oil
2 medium zucchini, sliced
2 sticks celery, sliced
250 g button mushrooms, sliced
4 cloves garlic, crushed
1 teaspoon sambal oelek
2/3 cup orange juice
1/3 cup plum sauce
2 tablespoons sherry
2 tablespoons teriyaki sauce

1. Slice beef evenly across the grain into flat, thin strips. Heat oil in frying pan or wok; add beef in batches and stir-fry over high heat 2–3 minutes or until browned but not cooked through. Remove from pan; drain on paper towels.
2. Add carrot and sesame oil to pan; stir-fry over high heat 2 minutes. Add zucchini, celery, mushrooms, garlic and sambal oelek, stir-fry 3 minutes.
3. Add orange juice, plum sauce, sherry and teriyaki sauce; stir-fry over high heat 2 minutes or until vegetables are soft and sauce has thickened. Return beef to pan; stir-fry 1 minute to heat through. Garnish with carrot strips, if desired.

Chicken, Mushroom and Vermicelli

Preparation time: 25 minutes
Total cooking time: 10 minutes
Serves 4

100 g vermicelli
12 large Chinese dried mushrooms
2 tablespoons oil
1 onion, chopped
2 cloves garlic, crushed
1–2 teaspoons sambal oelek
500 g chicken mince
2 cups bean sprouts
1/2 cup chopped fresh coriander
2 tablespoons lime juice
1 tablespoon fish sauce
1 tablespoon soy sauce

1. Cook vermicelli in large pan of rapidly boiling water 3 minutes or until just tender; drain well.
2. Place mushrooms in medium bowl; cover with boiling water. Stand 15 minutes or until soft, drain. Slice mushrooms; discard stems.
3. Heat oil in pan; add onion, garlic and sambal oelek. Stir over medium-high heat 2 minutes or until onion is almost soft. Add chicken; stir-fry over high heat 3 minutes until mince has browned and any liquid has evaporated. Use a fork to break up lumps of mince as it cooks.
4. Add sprouts, coriander, lime juice, fish sauce, soy sauce, cooked vermicelli and sliced mushrooms; stir over heat 2 minutes or until heated through. Garnish with sliced chilli, if desired.

> **Hint**
> When making a stir-fry, prepare all the ingredients first so that they are ready to be added to the pan quickly; chop vegetables into same sized pieces so that they cook evenly.

Chicken, Mushroom and Vermicelli (top)
Sweet and Spicy Steak and Vegetables

Fried Rice

Preparation time: 15 minutes
Total cooking time: 10 minutes
Serves 4

4 spring onions
2 tablespoons peanut oil
2 eggs, lightly beaten
1 medium onion, sliced
250 g sliced leg ham
4 cups cold, cooked rice
1/4 cup frozen peas
2 tablespoons soy sauce
250 g cooked small prawns, peeled

1. Cut spring onions into short diagonal lengths. Heat a tablespoon oil in a large frying pan or wok and add eggs. As egg begins to set, pull it towards the centre and tilt the pan to let the unset egg run to the edges.
2. When the egg has almost set, transfer it to a plate. Cut the egg into strips and set the strips aside.
3. Heat remaining oil in wok. Add onion and stir-fry over high heat 1–2 minutes or until it starts to turn transparent. Add ham; stir-fry 1 minute. Add rice and peas; stir-fry 3 minutes or until rice has heated through. Add eggs, soy, spring onion and prawns. Heat through; serve.

Chilli Octopus

Preparation time: 20 minutes + 2 hours marinating
Total cooking time: 4 minutes
Serves 4

750 g baby octopus
1 tablespoon oil
2 cloves garlic, crushed
2 tablespoons sweet chilli sauce
1 tablespoon lime juice
2 tablespoons oil, extra

1. Wash octopus thoroughly and wipe dry with a paper towel. Use a small sharp knife to slit open the head; remove the gut. Grasp body firmly and push beak out with your index finger; discard beak. If octopus are large, cut the tentacles in half.
2. Combine octopus, oil, garlic, sauce and juice in a bowl. Cover with plastic wrap and refrigerate 2 hours.
3. Heat extra oil in heavy-based frying pan or wok. Drain octopus, reserving marinade. Stir-fry octopus over medium heat for 3–4 minutes or until tender. Add reserved marinade and stir through until hot.

Five-spice Beef

Preparation time: 15 minutes
Total cooking time: 10 minutes
Serves 4

1 teaspoon five-spice powder
1/2 teaspoon black pepper
500 g rump steak
2 tablespoons oil
3 teaspoons finely grated ginger
4 spring onions, cut into 3 cm lengths
2 tablespoons soy sauce
2 tablespoons oyster sauce

1. Combine five-spice powder and pepper. Rub mixture into both sides of the meat. Cut meat into thin strips. Heat 1 tablespoon oil in heavy-based frying pan or wok. Stir-fry ginger and spring onion 1 minute. Remove from pan; keep warm.
2. Stir-fry meat in small batches over a high heat until just browned.
3. Return all meat to pan and add sauces; toss well. Serve immediately.

From top: Five-spice Beef, Chilli Octopus and Fried Rice

Spicy Lamb

Preparation time:
5 minutes
Total cooking time:
10 minutes
Serves 4

500 g lamb fillets
2 tablespoons oil
2 tablespoons ground cumin
2 teaspoons ground coriander
2 teaspoons dried mint
1 teaspoon turmeric
10 spinach leaves, shredded
2 teaspoons cornflour
1 tablespoon lemon juice
1/2 cup sultanas
1/4 cup pine nuts
yoghurt, for serving

1. Trim meat of fat and sinew; cut into strips. Heat oil in wok or frying pan. Add cumin, coriander, mint and turmeric and stir-fry over high heat 1 minute.
2. Add meat and stir-fry in batches over high heat 4 minutes, or until browned. Set aside on plate. Add spinach and stir-fry 4 minutes or until spinach is cooked.
3. Blend cornflour and juice. Stir into pan, add sultanas and pine nuts; stir-fry until sauce has thickened. Return meat to pan; stir to reheat. Remove from heat and top with a dollop of yoghurt.

Chinese-style Mixed Vegetables

Preparation time:
5 minutes
Total cooking time:
4 minutes
Serves 4

1 medium carrot
1 medium red capsicum
125 g green beans
1 tablespoon oil
1 clove garlic, crushed
200 g straw mushrooms
1 1/2 teaspoons cornflour
1/3 cup chicken stock
1 teaspoon sesame oil
1 teaspoon caster sugar
2 teaspoons soy sauce

1. Slice carrot finely. Seed capsicum and cut into medium pieces. Top and tail beans; cut in half.
2. Heat oil in a wok or heavy-based frying pan. Add carrot and stir-fry over high heat 30 seconds. Add garlic, capsicum, beans and mushrooms and stir-fry over high heat 2 minutes or until cooked but crisp.
3. Dissolve cornflour in a little of the stock. Mix with remaining stock, sesame oil, sugar and soy. Add to wok; stir until sauce thickens.

Spicy Chicken and Tomato Stir-fry

Preparation time:
15 minutes
Total cooking time:
8 minutes
Serves 4

2 tablespoons oil
2 cloves garlic, crushed
3 teaspoons chopped fresh rosemary
2 small red chillies, chopped
6 spring onions, chopped
500 g chicken breast fillets, cut into strips
1 large tomato, peeled, seeded, chopped
1 tablespoon tomato paste
1 tablespoon worcestershire sauce
3 teaspoons horseradish cream
freshly ground black pepper, to taste
1 tablespoon lemon juice

1. Heat oil in frying pan or wok; add garlic, rosemary, chilli and spring onion; stir-fry over high heat 2 minutes.
2. Add chicken; stir-fry 3 minutes or until lightly golden. Add tomato, tomato paste, sauce and horseradish; stir over heat 1 minute.
3. Add pepper and juice, stir over heat 2 minutes.

From top: Spicy Lamb, Spicy Chicken and Tomato Stir-fry and Chinese-style Mixed Vegetables

Café

Plum Pork and Vegetables

Preparation time:
15 minutes
Total cooking time:
10 minutes
Serves 4

500 g pork fillet
1 tablespoon oil
2 small onions, cut in wedges
2 teaspoons grated ginger
1/2 cup plum jam
2 tablespoons soy sauce
200 g snow peas, trimmed
2 small carrots, sliced diagonally
2 small parsnips, cut in strips

1. Trim meat of fat and sinew. Slice meat thinly Heat oil in frying pan or wok. Add meat and stir-fry over high heat 4 minutes or until browned; drain on paper towels.
2. Add onion and ginger and stir-fry over high heat 2 minutes or until golden. Add jam and soy sauce to pan; stir 2 minutes or until the jam has melted and thickened slightly.
3. Add snow peas, carrots and parsnips to pan and stir-fry over high heat 4 minutes. Return meat to pan and stir-fry over high heat 1 minute or until heated through. Remove from heat; serve immediately with rice or noodles.

Chinese Greens

Preparation time:
10 minutes
Total cooking time:
3 minutes
Serves 4–6

1 bunch baby bok choy or choi sum
1 tablespoon peanut oil
1 tablespoon oyster sauce
2 teaspoons black bean sauce
1 teaspoon sesame oil

1. Remove and discard any discoloured leaves and tough stems from bok choy. Separate leaves and wash thoroughly; pat dry with paper towels.
2. Cut stems into uniform lengths and leaves into wide strips. Heat oil in a wok; add stems. Stir fry briefly, then cover and cook 2 minutes. Add leaves and stir-fry 1 minute or until just tender.
3. Add sauces and sesame oil; stir 30 seconds or until heated through. Serve immediately.

Chicken and Bamboo Shoots

Preparation time:
30 minutes
Total cooking time:
10 minutes
Serves 4

1 tablespoon oil
4 spring onions, cut into 1 cm lengths
2 teaspoons finely grated ginger
500 g chicken breast fillet, sliced
1/2 cup bamboo shoots, sliced
1 red capsicum, thinly sliced
2 tablespoons soy sauce
1–2 tablespoons sweet chilli sauce
100 g roasted cashews

1. Heat oil in large frying pan or wok. Stir-fry spring onion and ginger over high heat 30 seconds. Add chicken and stir-fry in small batches over high heat 2–3 minutes or until chicken has browned but not cooked through.
2. Add bamboo shoots and capsicum; stir-fry over high heat 2 minutes. Add soy, chilli sauce and cashews and stir until heated through.

From top: Chinese Greens, Chicken and Bamboo Shoots, Plum Pork and Vegetables

Scallop and Vegetable Stir-fry

Preparation time:
15 minutes
Total cooking time:
8 minutes
Serves 4

2 tablespoons oil
500 g scallops
300 g sugar snap peas
250 g asparagus, cut into thin straws, 4 cm long
2 cloves garlic, crushed
4 spring onions, chopped
2 teaspoons ground turmeric
1/2 teaspoon dried chilli flakes
1/3 cup fish stock
1/4 cup sherry
1 tablespoon soy sauce
1/2 cup unsalted peanuts

1. Heat 1 tablespoon oil in frying pan or wok. Add scallops, stir-fry over high heat 1 minute or until lightly golden. Remove from pan; drain on paper towels.
2. Heat remaining oil in pan; add peas and asparagus and stir-fry over high heat 3 minutes or until almost tender. Add garlic, spring onion, turmeric and chilli; stir-fry 1 minute.
3. Add stock, sherry and soy sauce, stir over heat 1 minute or until vegetables are tender. Add peanuts and scallops; stir 1 minute or until heated through.

Thai-style Chicken

Preparation time:
20 minutes
Total cooking time:
10 minutes
Serves 4

350 g broccoli
1 medium red capsicum
1 medium onion
2 tablespoons oil
1 tablespoon green curry paste
2 stalks lemon grass, finely chopped
2 cloves garlic, crushed
500 g chicken breast fillet, sliced
1 tablespoon fish sauce
2 teaspoons lime juice
2 teaspoons soft brown sugar
1 tablespoon sweet chilli sauce

1. Trim stem of broccoli and cut into florets. Remove the seeds and membrane from capsicum and cut the flesh diagonally into 3 or 4 pieces. Cut onion into 8 segments and separate the pieces. Heat 1 tablespoon oil in a large frying pan or wok. Add curry paste, lemon grass and garlic; stir-fry over medium heat 30 seconds or until fragrant. Add onion, stir-fry another minute.
2. Add chicken and stir-fry in batches over high heat until browned but not cooked through. Remove from pan.
3. Heat remaining oil and add broccoli and capsicum. Stir-fry over high heat for 1 minute. Return chicken to pan; add fish sauce, juice and sugar and stir-fry 5 minutes over medium heat, or until chicken is cooked. Stir through sauce. Serve with sliced chilli, if desired.

> **Hint**
> Green curry paste is available in most supermarkets. It is made from green chillies and is quite hot. Use less than the amount suggested in the recipe if hotness is not to your taste. The flavour will not be affected.

Thai-style Chicken (top) and Scallop and Vegetable Stir-fry

Tofu and Vegetables

Preparation time:
20 minutes
Total cooking time:
20 minutes
Serves 4–6

125 g rice vermicelli
3/4 cup oil
1 tablespoon soy sauce
1 tablespoon sherry
1 tablespoon oyster sauce
1/2 cup chicken stock
2 teaspoons cornflour
2 teaspoons water
1 tablespoon oil, extra
1 clove garlic, crushed
1 teaspoon grated ginger
375 g firm tofu, cut into small cubes
2 medium carrots, cut into matchsticks
250 g snow peas, trimmed
4 spring onions, finely sliced
425 g can straw mushrooms, drained

1. Break vermicelli into short lengths. Heat half the oil in wok. Cook vermicelli in batches, over medium heat, until crisp, adding more oil when necessary. Drain on paper towels.
2. Combine soy sauce, sherry, oyster sauce and chicken stock. Blend cornflour with water.
3. Heat wok; add extra oil, garlic and ginger and cook over high heat 1 minute. Add tofu; stir-fry 3 minutes. Remove from wok. Add carrot and snow-peas; stir-fry 1 minute. Add combined sauces and stock; cover and cook another 3 minutes or until vegetables are tender but still crisp. Return tofu to pan.
4. Add spring onion, mushrooms and blended cornflour. Stir until the sauce has thickened; remove from heat. Serve with rice vermicelli.

Tofu and Vegetables

1 Cook vermicelli in hot oil and drain on paper towels.

2 Combine soy sauce, sherry, oyster sauce and chicken stock.

3 Stir-fry tofu cubes for 3 minutes or until well browned.

4 Return all ingredients to pan, add spring onion and mushrooms.

Noodles with Pork and Prawns

Preparation time:
20 minutes
Total cooking time:
10 minutes
Serves 4

12 medium cooked prawns
200 g roast or Chinese barbecued pork
500 g fresh thick egg noodles
1/4 cup peanut oil
2 teaspoons finely chopped garlic
1 tablespoon black bean sauce
1 tablespoon soy sauce
1 tablespoon bottled chilli and ginger sauce, optional
1 tablespoon white vinegar
1/4 cup chicken stock
125 g fresh bean sprouts, tails removed
3 spring onions, finely sliced
1/4 cup chopped fresh coriander, for garnish

1. Peel and devein prawns, leaving tails intact. Cut pork evenly into thin slices. Cook noodles in a large pan of rapidly boiling water until just tender; drain and set aside.
2. Heat oil in frying pan or wok. Add garlic, stir-fry over high heat 20 seconds. Add prawns and pork; stir-fry 1 minute. Add the noodles to the wok with sauces, vinegar and stock. Stir-fry over high heat 2–3 minutes or until mixture has heated through and sauce has been absorbed.
3. Add bean sprouts and spring onion and stir 1 minute. Transfer to serving dish; garnish with coriander.

Beef in Black Bean Sauce

Preparation time:
20 minutes
Total cooking time:
10 minutes
Serves 4

2 tablespoons salted black beans
1 medium onion
1 small red capsicum
1 small green capsicum
2 teaspoons cornflour
1/2 cup beef stock
2 teaspoons soy sauce
1 teaspoon sugar
2 tablespoons oil
1 teaspoon finely crushed garlic
1/4 teaspoon ground black pepper
400 g rump or fillet steak, finely sliced

1. Rinse black beans in several changes of water. Drain and mash beans. Cut the onion into wedges. Halve capsicums; discard seeds and cut into large pieces. Blend cornflour with stock; add soy and sugar.
2. Heat 1 tablespoon of the oil in a frying pan or wok; add garlic, pepper, onion and capsicum and stir-fry over high heat 1 minute, then transfer to a bowl.
3. Heat remaining oil; add beef strips and stir-fry over high heat 2 minutes or until meat browns. Add black beans, blended cornflour mixture and vegetables; stir until sauce boils and thickens.

HINT
Always heat the oil in the wok or frying pan before stir-frying—especially when cooking meat. The hot oil will sear the meat, capturing the juices.

Noodles with Pork and Prawns (top) and Beef in Black Bean Sauce

Chilli Noodle and Cashew Stir-fry

Preparation time:
20 minutes
Total cooking time:
5 minutes
Serves 4

200 g thin noodles, chopped
1/4 cup oil
2 teaspoons chilli oil
3 small red chillies, finely chopped
1/2 cup unsalted, roasted cashews
1 red capsicum, chopped
2 sticks celery, sliced diagonally
225 g can whole baby corn, drained and halved
100 g bean sprouts
1 tablespoon soy sauce
2 tablespoons sweet chilli sauce
2 tablespoons chopped spring onion

1. Cook noodles in pan of simmering water until just tender; drain.
2. Heat oils in frying pan or wok; add chilli and stir-fry over medium heat 1 minute. Add cashews; stir-fry 1 minute or until golden.
3. Add vegetables to pan; cook over medium heat 3 minutes or until vegetables are just tender. Stir in noodles and combined sauces. Toss until noodles have heated through and all ingredients are combined. Serve immediately sprinkled with the chopped spring onion.

Sesame Orange Beef

Preparation time:
15 minutes + 20 minutes refrigeration
Total cooking time:
10 minutes
Serves 4

400 g rump steak
2 teaspoons finely grated orange rind
2 teaspoons sesame oil
3/4 cup orange juice
1 1/2 teaspoons cornflour
2 tablespoons peanut oil
1 small onion, cut into eighths
2 small carrots, cut into sticks
150 g snake beans, cut into 5 cm lengths
1 tablespoon toasted sesame seeds
1 tablespoon soy sauce
1 tablespoon sesame oil, extra

1. Trim meat of excess fat and sinew. Cut across the grain into thin strips. Place in a non-metal dish with grated orange rind and sesame oil. Use your fingers to rub the flavourings into meat. Cover with plastic wrap and refrigerate 20 minutes. Combine the orange juice and cornflour; set aside.
2. Heat oil in frying pan or wok. Stir-fry meat in batches over high heat until browned. Set aside on a plate and keep warm.
3. Reheat pan: add onion, carrot and beans. Stir-fry 2 minutes over high heat or until just tender. Add cornflour mixture to pan, and stir until sauce boils and thickens. Return meat to pan; add sesame seeds, soy and sesame oil and stir until heated. Serve immediately.

> **HINT**
> Sesame oil is very strongly flavoured, so a little bit will go a long way. It is used primarily in marinades or for extra flavouring once the dish is cooked.

Chilli Noodle and Cashew Stir-fry (top)
Sesame Orange Beef

Pan-fried dishes

With some fresh ingredients, a few moments and a sturdy frying pan, a delicious meal is almost at hand. Pan-fried dishes can be dressed up for a dinner party or do equally well as a quick bistro-style supper. Either way, they should be served straight away—from the pan to the table. The accent is on speed and freshness.

Beef with Honey and Mustard Glaze

Preparation time:
5 minutes
Total cooking time:
15 minutes
Serves 4

1 tablespoon oil
4 beef eye fillet steaks
2 teaspoons grated fresh ginger
2 cloves garlic, crushed
1/2 cup beef stock
1/3 cup honey
2 tablespoons chopped fresh coriander
1 1/2 tablespoons Dijon mustard
1 tablespoon soy sauce
fresh chopped parsley, to serve

1. Heat oil in pan; add steaks. Cook over high heat 2 minutes each side to seal, turning once. For a rare result, cook another minute each side. For medium and well-done, reduce heat to medium; cook another 2–3 minutes each side for medium and 4–6 minutes each side for well-done. Remove meat from pan; keep warm.
2. Add ginger, garlic, stock, honey, coriander, mustard and soy sauce to pan; bring to the boil. Reduce heat to medium; simmer, uncovered, 4 minutes or until the sauce has reduced and thickened, stirring often. Pour sauce over steaks and sprinkle with parsley.

Beef with Honey and Mustard Glaze (top) and Lamb Cutlets with Rosemary and Butter Bean Sauce (recipe page 36)

Lamb Cutlets with Rosemary and Butter Bean Sauce

Preparation time:
10 minutes
Total cooking time:
5 minutes
Serves 4

310 g can butter beans
2 cloves garlic, crushed
2 tablespoons sour cream
1 tablespoon lemon juice
1 teaspoon ground paprika
2 tablespoons oil
1 tablespoon chopped fresh rosemary
8 lamb cutlets

1. Combine drained beans, garlic, sour cream, lemon juice and paprika in food processor or blender. Process for 30 seconds or until smooth.
2. Heat oil and rosemary in pan; add cutlets. Cook over high heat 2 minutes on each side for a rare result, turning once. For a medium result, cook another minute each side. Remove from pan, drain on paper towels; keep warm. Drain excess fat from pan.
3. Add reserved bean puree to pan, stir over heat 1 minute or until heated through. Serve immediately with cutlets.

Pork Chops with Redcurrant Glaze

Preparation time:
10 minutes
Total cooking time:
20 minutes
Serves 4

4 pork loin chops
1 tablespoon oil
1 cup white wine
1/3 cup redcurrant jelly

1. Trim meat of excess fat and sinew. Heat oil in heavy-based pan; add chops. Cook over medium heat 8 minutes each side, or until tender and browned. Remove chops from pan and keep warm.
2. Add wine and jelly to pan; stir to combine with pan juices. Bring sauce to the boil and simmer 10 minutes or until reduced by half. Pour over chops.

> **HINT**
> Wipe out pan with paper towels while it is still warm—this makes it easier to clean.

Swiss Rosti

Preparation time:
10 minutes
Total cooking time:
40 minutes
Serves 4

700 g potatoes
1/2 teaspoon salt
pepper, to taste
1 tablespoon oil
30 g butter

1. Peel potatoes and grate on a coarse grater; firmly squeeze out excess moisture. Drain potato flesh on paper towels and sprinkle with salt and pepper.
2. Heat oil and half the butter in medium heavy-based frying pan. Add potato; press down firmly. Cook, without stirring, over low heat 20 minutes or until potato has browned and is crusty underneath. Slide onto a plate and keep warm. Heat remaining butter in pan; when sizzling, return potato cake to pan cooked-side up. Cook over medium heat 10 minutes or until potatoes have browned and underside is crusty. Cut into wedges to serve. Serve with bread and a crisp green salad, if desired.

Swiss Rosti (top) and Pork Chops with Redcurrant Glaze

1 Add mushrooms to pan and cook, stirring, until soft.

2 Add cheese to risotto when it is ready to remove from heat.

Mushroom Risotto Fritters

Preparation time:
20 minutes + 1 hour 15 minutes refrigeration
Total cooking time:
30 minutes
Serves 4

3 1/4 cups vegetable stock
1 tablespoon olive oil
20 g butter
1 small onion, finely chopped
1 cup arborio or short grain rice
150 g small button mushrooms, thinly sliced
1/3 cup freshly grated parmesan cheese
oil, for frying

1. Bring stock to the boil in a small pan. Reduce heat; cover and simmer slowly until needed. Heat oil and butter in heavy-based pan. Add onion; stir over medium heat 3 minutes or until softened. Add rice; cook 2 minutes. Add mushrooms and cook 3 minutes or until soft.
2. Add hot stock 1/2 a cup at a time, stirring constantly, until all stock is absorbed. Repeat process until all the stock has been added and rice is just tender and creamy, stirring constantly. (This will take about 20 minutes.) Stir in cheese and remove from heat.
3. Transfer mixture to a bowl to cool; refrigerate for at least 1 hour. With wetted hands, shape 1/4 cupfuls of mixture into flat rounds. Refrigerate 15 minutes.
4. Heat about 2 cm oil in a non-stick pan. Cook fritters 3–4 minutes each side, until golden and crisp. Drain on paper towels. Serve with relish, if desired.

Mushroom Risotto Fritters

3 Using wetted hands, shape refrigerated risotto mixture into flat rounds.

4 Cook fritters 3–4 minutes each side, then drain on paper towels.

Aromatic Pork Pan-fry

Preparation time:
15 minutes
Total cooking time:
25 minutes
Serves 4

2 pork fillets (500 g)
1/4 cup oil
1 large onion, finely chopped
1 large green apple, peeled, cored and finely diced
1/2 teaspoon yellow mustard seeds
2 teaspoons curry powder
1 teaspoon grated fresh ginger
1 cinnamon stick
500 g ripe tomatoes, peeled and roughly diced
1/2 teaspoon salt
1/2 cup yoghurt
1 tablespoon finely chopped fresh mint

1. Trim pork fillets of sinew and cut into diagonal strips. Heat half the oil in large pan; add pork and cook 2–3 minutes or until browned. Remove from pan and keep warm. Heat remaining oil in pan; add onion and apple. Cook 5 minutes or until browned.
2. Add mustard seeds; cook 1 minute or until seeds begin to pop. Add curry powder, ginger and cinnamon stick; fry until fragrant. Add pork, tomatoes and salt. Cover and cook gently 15 minutes or until the pork is tender and cooked through.
3. Add the yoghurt and mint just before serving. Heat, but do not boil.

Pepper Steak with Brandy Sauce

Preparation time:
15 minutes
Total cooking time:
10 minutes
Serves 4

2 tablespoons pink peppercorns
2 tablespoons white peppercorns
2 tablespoons black peppercorns
2 teaspoons salt
2 tablespoons oil
4 fillet steaks, trimmed of excess fat

Brandy Sauce
6 cloves garlic, crushed
1/4 cup brandy
1 cup thickened or pouring cream

Aromatic Pork Pan-fry (top) and Pepper Steak with Brandy Sauce

1. Crush peppercorns in a food processor or place in a paper bag and crush with a rolling pin. Combine in a bowl with salt and oil. Press the mixture firmly into each steak with your fingers.
2. Heat a heavy-based frying pan over high heat; add steaks. Reduce heat to moderately high and cook 2–3 minutes. Turn steaks over, being careful not to dislodge pepper crust, and cook 2–3 minutes on other side. (Steaks should be medium rare.) Transfer steaks to large platter and keep warm.
3. To make brandy sauce: Combine garlic and brandy in pan and cook over high heat 1 minute. Add cream and cook over medium heat, stirring constantly 3–4 minutes or until sauce is thick enough to coat the back of a spoon. Drizzle sauce over each steak to serve. Serve with roast potatoes, pumpkin and green beans, if desired.

Hint
If serving rice with any pan-fried dish, drizzle a little of the sauce for the meat over the rice and stir through. This will keep it moist and add flavour.

Leek, Zucchini and Cheese Frittata

Preparation time:
20 minutes
Total cooking time:
40 minutes
Serves 4

2 tablespoons olive oil
3 leeks, thinly sliced
2 medium zucchini, cut into matchstick pieces
1 clove garlic, crushed
salt and pepper, to taste
5 eggs, lightly beaten
1/3 cup grated parmesan cheese
1/3 cup Swiss cheese, cut into small cubes

1. Heat 1 tablespoon olive oil in small pan; add leek and cook, stirring, until slightly softened. Place a lid on pan; cook for 10 minutes. Add zucchini and garlic; cook another 10 minutes. Transfer to a bowl. Cool; add salt, pepper, egg and cheeses.
2. Heat remaining oil in pan; add mixture and smooth surface. Cook over low heat for 15 minutes or until frittata is almost set.
3. Cook under preheated hot grill 3–5 minutes or until top is set and golden. Stand frittata 5 minutes before cutting into wedges to serve.

Herb-crusted Tuna Steaks

Preparation time:
15 minutes + 15 minutes refrigeration
Total cooking time:
10 minutes
Serves 4

1 cup combined chopped fresh herbs
8 slices day-old bread, crusts removed
1 egg
2 tablespoons milk
4 tuna steaks
2 tablespoons olive oil
salt and pepper, to taste

1. Place herbs and bread in food processor; process 30 seconds or until mixture is very fine. Whisk egg and milk in a small bowl.
2. Dip each tuna steak in the egg mixture, then coat evenly with herb breadcrumbs, pressing firmly with fingers. Refrigerate 15 minutes.
3. Heat oil in heavy-based pan; cook tuna 2 minutes each side over high heat. Season to taste and serve immediately with green salad, if desired.

Leek, Zucchini and Cheese Frittata (top) and Herb-crusted Tuna Steaks

Steak and Onions

Preparation time:
10 minutes
Total cooking time:
20 minutes
Serves 4

4 pieces fillet or rump steak
2 large onions
30 g butter
2 cloves garlic, finely chopped
1/2 teaspoon sugar
salt and pepper, to taste
1 tablespoon oil
2 tablespoons barbecue sauce
2 tablespoons finely chopped parsley

1. Trim steaks of excess fat and sinew. Peel onions; cut in half and slice thinly. Melt butter in large frying pan. Add onions; cook over low heat 5 minutes or until softened, stirring occasionally. Add garlic and sugar; cook for 2 minutes. Transfer to a warmed plate lined with paper towels; season and cover with foil to keep warm.
2. Heat oil in pan; add steaks. Cook 3–4 minutes each side to sear. Spread each steak with a little barbecue sauce; top with warm onion mixture. Cook, without turning, another 3 minutes for a rare result or another 5 minutes for medium. Sprinkle with parsley and serve steak with chips, if desired.

Rissoles in Barbecue Gravy

Preparation time:
20 minutes + 30 minutes refrigeration
Total cooking time:
20 minutes
Serves 6–8

750 g beef mince
250 g sausage mince
1 small onion, finely chopped
1 tablespoon worcestershire sauce
2 tablespoons tomato sauce
1 cup fresh breadcrumbs
1 egg, lightly beaten

Barbecue Gravy
1 small onion, finely chopped
2 tablespoons plain flour
1 tablespoon brown vinegar
1 tablespoon soft brown sugar
1/3 cup tomato sauce
1 tablespoon worcestershire sauce
1 cup beef stock

1. Place beef mince and sausage mince in large bowl; add onion, sauces, breadcrumbs and egg. Using hands, mix until thoroughly combined. Divide mixture into 6 equal portions and shape into thick patties. Refrigerate 30 minutes.
2. Heat pan and brush lightly with oil. Cook patties over medium heat 7 minutes each side, turning once. Transfer to a plate; cover with foil and keep warm.
3. To make barbecue gravy: Add onion to pan; cook over medium heat 5 minutes or until soft. Stir in flour and cook 1 minute. Gradually add combined vinegar, sugar, sauces and stock. Bring to the boil and simmer 2 minutes, stirring occasionally. Serve gravy over the rissoles.

> HINT
> Rissoles can be cooked on a barbecue grill or flatplate. Make sure the fire is very hot, but glowing rather than flaming, and place rissoles over the hottest part of the fire, searing quickly on both sides.

Steak and Onions (top) and Rissoles in Barbecue Gravy

Peppered Lamb Fillet with Raisin Sauce

Preparation time:
15 minutes
Total cooking time:
20 minutes
Serves 4

600 g lamb fillets
1 tablespoon black pepper
1 tablespoon oil
4 spring onions, chopped
2 tablespoons raisins
2 tablespoons whisky
2 teaspoons chopped fresh thyme
1 cup thickened or pouring cream
salt, to taste

1. Trim fat and any silver sinew from fillets. Using your fingertips, rub fillets with pepper. Heat oil in a heavy-based frying pan. Cook fillets, 2 or 3 at a time, over medium heat 3–4 minutes, turning occasionally. Transfer meat to a warmed plate, cover with foil to keep warm.
2. Return pan to heat; cook spring onions and raisins 2 minutes. Pour in whisky and allow liquid to almost evaporate; add thyme and cream and simmer 2 minutes, stirring occasionally.
3. Cut meat into diagonal slices and arrange on warmed serving plates. Spoon sauce over meat, season with salt and serve immediately. Serve with steamed vegetables, if desired.

Veal Schnitzel

Preparation time:
20 minutes + 30 minutes refrigeration
Total cooking time:
4–6 minutes
Serves 4

4 veal steaks
1/3 cup plain flour
2 eggs, lightly beaten
1/2 cup breadcrumbs
1/3 cup oil
50 g cheddar cheese, thinly sliced
1 cup bottled tomato-based pasta sauce

1. Trim meat of excess fat and sinew. Flatten steaks to an even thickness, nicking edges to prevent meat curling. Spread flour over a sheet of greaseproof paper. Coat meat lightly in flour; shake off excess flour. Dip steaks, one at a time, into egg. Coat meat with breadcrumbs, pressing firmly with fingers and shaking off excess crumbs. Arrange meat in a single layer on a large plate; cover with plastic wrap. Refrigerate for 30 minutes.
2. Heat oil in heavy-based pan. Cook veal over medium heat for 2–3 minutes. Turn meat over and lay cheese slices on cooked side. Cook for another 2–3 minutes; lift from pan with a slotted spatula and drain on paper towels.
3. Warm pasta sauce in microwave or small pan. Place meat on serving plates and top with sauce.

Veal Schnitzel (top) and Peppered Lamb Fillet with Raisin Sauce

> **HINT**
> The secret of schnitzel is to use very thin meat. When pounding meat to an even thickness, cover the meat with plastic wrap, so that the mallet will not tear the meat. Use the side of the mallet, rather than the toothed head, if the meat is already thin, but needs some evening out.

Spicy Eggplant Slices

Preparation time:
15 minutes +
15 minutes standing
Total cooking time:
10 minutes
Serves 4–6

2 medium eggplant (250 g each)
salt
1/3 cup plain flour
2 teaspoons ground cumin
2 teaspoons ground coriander
1 teaspoon chilli powder
oil, for frying
1/2 cup plain yoghurt
1 tablespoon chopped fresh mint

1. Cut eggplant into 1 cm slices. Arrange in a single layer on a tray and cover well with salt. Leave to stand for 15 minutes, then rinse and pat dry thoroughly with paper towels.
2. Sift flour and spices onto a plate. Dust eggplant with flour mixture; shake off any excess.
3. Heat about 2 cm oil in heavy-based pan. Cook eggplant slices a few at a time, 2–3 minutes each side or until golden. Drain on paper towels. Combine yoghurt and mint. Serve with warm eggplant.

Ocean Trout with Basil Crème Fraîche

Preparation time:
10 minutes
Total cooking time:
12 minutes
Serves 4

1 tablespoon oil
30 g butter
4 ocean trout fillets
2 leeks, thinly sliced
1/2 cup dry white wine
1/2 cup fish stock
1/2 cup crème fraîche or thick cream
1/4 cup sliced fresh basil leaves

1. Heat oil and butter in pan; add trout fillets. Cook 2 minutes on each side or until just cooked through. Remove trout from pan; cover with foil to keep warm.
2. Add leeks to pan; stir over medium-high heat 5 minutes or until soft. Add wine; cook mixture, uncovered, 2 minutes or until liquid has reduced by half. Add stock; cook until liquid has reduced by half again.
3. Add crème fraîche and basil, stir over heat 1 minute or until heated through. Spoon over trout to serve. Serve with salad, if desired.

Spicy Eggplant Slices (top)
Ocean Trout with Basil Crème Fraîche

Hint
White fish fillets are also suitable for this recipe. Crème fraîche is made by combining 1 cup pure thick cream with 1/2 cup sour cream. Stand at room temperature 5–6 hours until slightly thickened. Cover and refrigerate. Will keep for around 10 days in an airtight container.

1 Combine the dry ingredients and make a well in the centre.

2 Use a wire whisk to stir the batter until just combined.

Fried Green Tomatoes

Preparation time: 10 minutes
Total cooking time: 12 minutes
Serves 4–6

3/4 cup plain flour
1 teaspoon salt
1/2 teaspoon white pepper
1/4 cup cornmeal
1 egg
3/4 cup milk
4 medium green tomatoes (500 g) (See Hint)
oil, for frying

1. Sift flour, salt and pepper into medium bowl. Add cornmeal and stir to combine. Make a well in the centre.
2. Combine egg and milk and add gradually to flour mixture. Whisk batter until just combined, but do not overbeat.
3. Cut tomatoes into thick slices. Heat about 1 cm oil in frying pan.
4. Dip tomatoes into batter; drain excess and fry 1 minute each side, turning once with tongs. Drain on paper towels and serve immediately.

HINT
Green tomatoes are simply tomatoes that have yet to ripen and turn red. Use half-green, half-red tomatoes if the green ones are difficult to find.

Fried Green Tomatoes

3 Cut the tomatoes into slices thick enough to fry.

4 Fry the battered tomatoes in hot oil several minutes, turning once.

Veal Steaks with Tomato, Olive and Anchovy Sauce

Preparation time: 15 minutes
Total cooking time: 15 minutes
Serves 4

1 tablespoon oil
8 small veal fillet (or scotch fillet) steaks
1 medium onion, chopped
2 cloves garlic, chopped
4 anchovy fillets, chopped
500 g ripe red tomatoes, chopped
1 tablespoon balsamic vinegar
salt and pepper, to taste
1/2 cup pitted black olives, halved
1 tablespoon chopped fresh parsley

1. Heat oil in a large heavy-based frying pan. Cook steaks over medium heat for 1–2 minutes each side. Transfer to a warmed plate; cover with foil and keep warm.
2. Add onion and garlic to pan; cook over low heat 5 minutes, stirring frequently. Add anchovies and tomato; cook for another 5 minutes. Stir in balsamic vinegar and season sauce with salt and pepper, to taste. Cook sauce 1 minute. Stir in olives and parsley; warm through.
3. Place veal steaks on warmed individual serving plates. Top veal with 2–3 tablespoons of sauce. Serve with pasta, if desired.

Chicken with Spicy Onion Sauce

Preparation time: 10 minutes
Total cooking time: 25 minutes
Serves 4

1/3 cup plain flour
1 teaspoon ground paprika
1 teaspoon ground turmeric
1 teaspoon ground cumin
1 teaspoon ground coriander
1/2 teaspoon ground chilli
1/2 teaspoon garlic salt
8 chicken thigh fillets, trimmed of fat
2 tablespoons oil
2 onions, cut into wedges
2 teaspoons grated fresh ginger
1/4 cup fruit chutney
1 cup chicken stock

1. Combine flour, paprika, turmeric, cumin, coriander, chilli and garlic salt in a medium bowl. Add chicken pieces and toss until well-coated in mixture; shake off the excess.
2. Heat half the oil in a heavy-based pan; add chicken. Cook over medium-high heat 3 minutes on each side or until golden brown; turn once during cooking. Remove chicken from the pan and drain on some paper towels.
3. Heat the remaining oil in the same pan; add onions and ginger to the pan. Stir over medium heat 3 minutes or until onion is tender. Add chutney and stock; stir until combined. Return chicken to pan; reduce heat to low. Cover pan with a lid and cook 15 minutes or until chicken is tender. Uncover and simmer another 5 minutes or until the sauce has reduced and thickened. Garnish with strips of spring onion and capsicum, if desired.

> **Hint**
> Quickly frying ground spices over high heat releases their flavours and fragrances.

Veal Steaks with Tomato, Olive and Anchovy Sauce (top) and Chicken with Spicy Onion Sauce

Orange Chicken

Preparation time: 15 minutes
Total cooking time: 50 minutes
Serves 4

30 g butter
1 tablespoon oil
8 chicken drumsticks
2 onions, sliced
2 cloves garlic, crushed
1/4 cup orange juice
2 teaspoons grated orange rind
1 teaspoon soft brown sugar
1/2 cup white wine
1/2 cup water
40 g French onion soup mix

1. Heat butter and oil in a heavy-based frying pan; add chicken. Cook over medium heat, turning occasionally, 5 minutes or until well browned. Remove chicken from pan and drain on paper towels.
2. Add onion and garlic to pan; stir over medium heat 3 minutes or until onion is tender. Add orange juice and rind, sugar, wine and combined water and soup mix; stir until combined.
3. Return chicken to pan; bring sauce to the boil. Reduce heat to low and cook, covered, 40 minutes or until chicken is tender and sauce has reduced and thickened. (Stir sauce occasionally as it cooks.) Serve with tomatoes and rice salad, if desired.

Lamb's Fry with Bacon

Preparation time: 10 minutes
Total cooking time: 30 minutes
Serves 6

1 lamb's liver (750 g)
1/4 cup cornflour
1/4 teaspoon ground black pepper
6 rashers bacon
2 tablespoons oil
2 medium onions, finely sliced
1 beef stock cube, crumbled
1 cup boiling water

1. Wash liver and slice thinly and evenly, discarding any veins or discoloured spots. Pat dry with paper towels. Combine cornflour and pepper on a sheet of greaseproof paper. Toss liver slices lightly in seasoned cornflour, shaking off excess.
2. Cut bacon into large pieces. Cook in a frying pan until crisp. Drain on paper towels. Add oil to pan; add onion and fry gently 5–10 minutes or until golden. Remove from pan with slotted spoon.

Lamb's Fry with Bacon (top) and Orange Chicken

3. Cook liver quickly in small batches over medium heat until well browned; remove from pan and drain on paper towels. Return liver, bacon and onion to pan. Dissolve the stock cube in boiling water; add blended stock gradually to pan. Stir over medium heat for 10 minutes or until the sauce boils and thickens. Serve with roast potatoes and steamed vegetables, if desired.

Hint
Liver is very high in vitamins A and B. One serving (150 g) provides more than the recommended daily intake of these vitamins.

Lemon and Rosemary Chicken

Preparation time: 10 minutes
Total cooking time: 30 minutes
Serves 4

30 g butter
1 tablespoon oil
4 chicken marylands, skin removed
2 small red chillies, finely chopped
1 tablespoon chopped fresh rosemary
6 cloves garlic, crushed
1/3 cup lemon juice
1/3 cup chicken stock
4 medium potatoes, peeled and cut into 3 cm cubes

1. Heat butter and oil in a frying pan; add chicken. Cook over medium heat 5 minutes or until well browned.
2. Add chillies, rosemary, garlic, lemon juice, stock and potatoes. Cover pan with a tight-fitting lid; reduce heat to very low. Cook, covered, for 25 minutes or until chicken and potatoes are tender. Stir occasionally during cooking and skim fat. Serve with steamed carrots, if desired.

Pork Steaks with Cider Ginger Sauce

Preparation time: 10 minutes
Total cooking time: 8 minutes
Serves 4

4 pork butterfly steaks
1 tablespoon oil
1 teaspoon grated ginger
1 cup cider
1 teaspoon cornflour
1 tablespoon chopped chives

1. Trim meat of any excess fat and sinew. Heat oil in a heavy-based pan; add meat. Cook over medium heat 2–3 minutes each side until tender, turning once. Remove from pan; keep warm.
2. Add ginger to pan, stirring and scraping with a wooden spoon. Place 1 tablespoon of the cider in a small bowl; add cornflour and stir until smooth. Combine with remaining cider. Add to pan; bring to the boil and simmer, stirring, 2 minutes, until sauce has thickened and reduced. Stir in chives. Serve sauce over steaks.

Lemon and Rosemary Chicken (top) and Pork Steaks with Cider Ginger Sauce

Spicy Steak

Preparation time: 5 minutes
Total cooking time: 10 minutes
Serves 4

4 fillet steaks
2 tablespoons cracked black pepper
2 teaspoons oil
1/2 cup chicken stock
1 tablespoon worcestershire sauce
1 tablespoon tomato sauce
1 teaspoon mild mustard
1/2 teaspoon dry, English-style hot mustard
1 clove crushed garlic
2 tablespoons finely chopped parsley
30 g butter

1. Trim steaks of excess fat. Firmly rub pepper into steaks. Heat oil in a large heavy-based pan. Add steaks; cook over high heat 3–5 minutes or until seared on both sides, turning once. Reduce heat to medium; for a rare result cook another minute, for medium cook another 2–3 minutes both sides or for well-done cook another 5 minutes both sides. Remove from pan and keep warm.
2. Add stock, sauces, mustards and garlic to pan; stir quickly, scraping bottom of pan with a wooden spoon. Bring sauce to boil; cook 30 seconds to reduce sauce slightly, then turn off heat. Add parsley and butter to sauce. Stir sauce until butter melts. Return steak to pan and warm through. Serve steak with sauteed potatoes and steamed green beans and sugar snap peas, if desired.

Spanish Omelette with Smoked Salmon

Preparation time: 15 minutes
Total cooking time: 35 minutes
Serves 4

1/4 cup oil
2 onions, finely chopped
375 g potato, peeled and cut into 1 cm cubes
salt and white pepper, to taste
125 g smoked salmon, finely chopped
2 tablespoons chopped fresh parsley
5 eggs, lightly beaten
1/4 cup pouring cream

1. Heat 2 tablespoons of the oil in a heavy-based frying pan; add onion and potato. Cook over medium heat, turning frequently, 5 minutes or until potatoes are golden. Reduce heat, cover the pan and cook another 5 minutes or until potato and onion are soft.
2. Transfer potato mixture to a bowl; add salmon and parsley to mixture. Add combined eggs and cream and stir to combine.
3. Add remaining oil to frying pan; pour in omelette mixture. Cook, over low heat, 10 minutes or until egg just begins to set on the surface. Place pan under preheated hot grill 1–2 minutes or until top has just set. (Omelette will set more on standing.) Stand several minutes in a warm place then cut into wedges to serve.

> **Hint**
> Use other smoked fish in this omelette such as smoked trout or mackerel. Canned salmon can also be used, as long as it is well drained and trimmed of any skin and bone.

Spicy Steak (top) and Spanish Omelette with Smoked Salmon

Fish with Coconut and Spices

Preparation time:
15 minutes
Total cooking time:
10 minutes
Serves 4

1 1/2 tablespoons oil
4 firm white fish fillets
1 tablespoon oil, extra
2 cloves garlic, crushed
2 teaspoons grated fresh ginger
4 spring onions, chopped
1 teaspoon ground cumin
1 teaspoon curry powder
1 teaspoon ground paprika
1 cup coconut milk
1 tablespoon lemon juice
2 tablespoons chopped fresh coriander

1. Heat oil in pan; add fish fillets. Cook over medium-high heat 2 minutes on each side or until just cooked. Remove from pan, drain on paper towels and keep warm.
2. Heat extra oil in pan; add garlic, ginger and spring onions. Stir over medium heat 2 minutes. Add cumin, curry and paprika; stir over heat 1 minute.
3. Add coconut milk and lemon juice to pan. Reduce heat to low; cook, uncovered, 3 minutes or until sauce has reduced and thickened, stirring often. Stir in coriander. Pour sauce over fish and serve immediately. Serve with a salad, if desired.

Curried Lamb Steaks

Preparation time:
15 minutes
Total cooking time:
10 minutes
Serves 4

2 tablespoons oil
500 g topside lamb steaks
2 onions, sliced
2 cloves garlic, crushed
2 teaspoons grated fresh ginger
1 small red chilli, chopped
1 tablespoon red curry paste
2 tablespoons lemon juice
1/2 cup lamb or chicken stock
2 tablespoons chopped fresh mint
2 tablespoons chopped fresh coriander

1. Heat oil in heavy-based pan; add lamb steaks. Cook over medium-high heat 4 minutes or until meat

Curried Lamb Steaks (top) and Fish with Coconut and Spices

is golden brown. Turn steaks once during cooking. Remove meat from pan, drain on paper towels, cover and keep warm.

2. Add onion, garlic, ginger and chilli; stir over medium heat 3 minutes or until onions are soft and tender. Add curry paste; stir over high heat 1 minute or until fragrant.

3. Add lemon juice, stock, mint and coriander; stir over medium heat 2 minutes or until sauce has reduced and thickened. Return lamb to sauce; reheat briefly. Serve with a fresh green salad, if desired.

Fish on Tomato Sauce

Preparation time:
15 minutes
Total cooking time:
20 minutes
Serves 4

1 tablespoon oil
1 clove garlic, crushed
1 small red capsicum, finely chopped
1 medium sized onion, finely chopped
500 g tomatoes, roughly chopped
salt and pepper, to taste
1 teaspoon sugar
1 teaspoon chilli sauce
1/4 cup water
4 white fish fillets
salt and pepper, extra, to taste
juice of 1/2 lemon
2 tablespoons finely chopped fresh coriander

1. Heat oil in large pan; add garlic, capsicum and onion. Cook over medium heat for 10 minutes or until soft, stirring occasionally. Add tomatoes, salt and pepper, sugar and chilli sauce. Reduce heat to low and cook for 10 minutes or until the sauce has reduced and thickened. Add the water and stir until hot.

2. Place fish over sauce in a single layer. Season with salt, pepper and lemon. Cover pan and cook over medium heat 5 minutes or until fish flakes when touched with a fork. Sprinkle with coriander.

Chicken with Creamy Herb and Mushroom Sauce

Preparation time:
15 minutes
Total cooking time:
10 minutes
Serves 4

2 tablespoons oil
4 chicken breast fillets
1 onion, cut into wedges
2 cloves garlic, crushed
250 g small field or button mushrooms
2/3 cup sour cream
1/2 cup chicken stock
2 tablespoons Dijon mustard
2 teaspoons lemon juice
2 tablespoons chopped fresh parsley
1 tablespoon chopped fresh oregano
1 tablespoon chopped fresh thyme

1. Heat oil in pan; add chicken. Cook over medium-high heat 3 minutes each side, turning once. Remove chicken from pan, drain on paper towels, cover and keep warm.

2. Add onion and garlic to pan; stir over medium heat 2 minutes or until onion is soft. Add mushrooms; stir over heat 2 minutes or until browned.

3. Add sour cream, stock, mustard, lemon juice, parsley, oregano and thyme. Cook over medium heat 2 minutes, stirring occasionally. Return chicken to pan; stir over heat 2–3 minutes or until just cooked through. Serve with hot noodles, if desired.

Hint
Pan-fried dishes should be served immediately, however some sauces, such as the Tomato Sauce, can be made a day or two ahead or even frozen for several weeks. You can make double the quantity of sauce and store for later.

Fish on Tomato Sauce (top) and Chicken with Creamy Herb and Mushroom Sauce

Index

Front cover: Beef and Bok Choy (right, recipe page 12) and Noodles with Pork and Prawns (left, recipe page 30).